The Life Cycle of Paper

© 2011 Discovery Communications, LLC. **Discovery Education**™ and the **Discovery Education** logo are trademarks of Discovery Communications, LLC, used under license. All rights reserved.

Conceived and produced by Weldon Owen Pty Ltd
59–61 Victoria Street, McMahons Point
Sydney NSW 2060, Australia

Copyright © 2011 Weldon Owen Pty Ltd

WELDON OWEN PTY LTD
Managing Director Kay Scarlett
Creative Director Sue Burk
Publisher Helen Bateman

**Senior Vice President,
International Sales** Stuart Laurence
Vice President Sales North America
Ellen Towell
**Administration Manager,
International Sales** Kristine Ravn

Editor Madeleine Jennings
Copy Editors Barbara McClenahan,
Bronwyn Sweeney, Shan Wolody
Editorial Assistant Natalie Ryan
Design Managers Michelle Cutler,
Kathryn Morgan
Designer Lore Foye
Images Manager Trucie Henderson
Picture Research Tracey Gibson
Pre-press Operator Linda Benton
Production Director Todd Rechner
Production and Pre-press Controller
Mike Crowton

Consultant Glenn Murphy

ISBN: 978-1-74252-157-2

Printed and bound in China by 1010 Printing Int Ltd.

A WELDON OWEN PRODUCTION

The Life Cycle of Paper

Meredith Costain

Contents

Paper products

People use paper products every day. Copy paper is used to print out a school project or a set of instructions. Books, newspapers, and magazines, all made from varying grades of paper, are read and enjoyed. Noses are blown on tissues, and paper towels are used to soak up spilled milk. Paper is used for products as different as food packaging, kitty litter, greeting cards, money, and wallpaper. It is even used to make clothing, chimneys, and coffins! In fact, more than 5,000 different products are made from paper or papermaking by-products.

Tissues
The paper used to make tissues is often treated with softeners, moisturizing agents, or perfume.

Origami paper
Traditional origami paper, used by the Japanese to create folded designs, is a heavy paper made from bark.

Newspapers and magazines
The USA produces 25 billion newspapers and 350 million magazines every year.

Gift wrap
Colorful wrapping paper is made from bleached softwood pulp. Fancy coatings are added during the printing process.

Paper lanterns
At festival times in Asian countries, paper lanterns fill the streets. They come in many different shapes and sizes. The simplest type is a paper bag with a candle inside. Others are much more complex, with bamboo or metal hoops covered with tough, colored paper.

History of papermaking

The word "paper" comes from the Egyptian word "papyrus." The ancient Egyptians wrote on mats made from papyrus reed, which were time–consuming and expensive to make. It was the Chinese who invented "true" paper, 3,000 years later.

THE BLACK PLAGUE

Early European paper was made from recycled clothing rags. Clothing from the millions of people killed by the Black Plague provided plenty of raw material.

3700–3200 BC	AD 105	300s–600s	700s	751	1400s
Ancient Egyptians cut thin strips from reeds and soften them to make papyrus.	A Chinese courtier, Ts'ai Lun, makes paper from mulberry bark, linen, and hemp.	Papermaking spreads to Vietnam, Tibet, Korea, Nepal, India, and Japan.	Empress Shotoku of Japan has millions of prayers printed on paper sheets.	Arabs learn papermaking from the Chinese. Paper use spreads into the Islamic world.	Germans and other Europeans make paper from recycled cotton and linen rags.

1452
Johannes Gutenberg prints the first book, using movable type.

late 1400s
The Aztecs independently invent paper, made from agave plant fibers.

1719
René de Réamur discovers paper can be made from wood, after watching wasps building nests.

late 1700s
Nicholas Robert creates a machine that can produce a seamless length of paper.

1838
Charles Fenerty makes the first paper from wood pulp, used for newspapers.

1870
Robert Gair invents the corrugated cardboard box, made in bulk.

Where does paper come from?

There are many different kinds of paper—smooth and white, pulpy and soft, mass-produced or handmade. All paper, however, is made from fibers from different materials that have been pressed together. Paper can be made from wheat straw, sugarcane stalks, rags, cotton, flax, and hemp. Most paper is made from wood fibers. Trees produce a large amount of fiber, and, compared with other materials, are cheap to grow.

Paper from rags
Paper made from rags is stronger and lasts longer than paper made from wood fibers. It can be made from recycled fabric or new cotton fibers.

Pine is a softwood.

Softwoods and hardwoods

Fibers from different types of trees are used to make different kinds of paper. Softwoods are used to make newspaper and tissue paper. Hardwoods are used for high-quality copy and writing paper.

Birch is a hardwood.

Softwood forests

Softwood trees, such as pine and spruce, are grown in managed plantations. To ensure sustainability, more trees are planted than are cut down. Only trees with a diameter smaller than 8 inches (20 cm), or that are unsuitable for solid wood products, are felled.

Logging

The process of cutting down trees is called logging. There are several different ways that trees can be logged. Clear-felling is when all the trees in an area of forest are removed. Select-felling is when only certain trees are removed, leaving the rest to continue to grow. Decisions about how a forest will be logged are made by forest managers. Chain saws are used to cut down trees marked for select-felling or that are difficult for logging machines to reach when clear-felling. For safety, each tree is cut so that it falls in a particular direction.

Clear-felling
All the trees in this clear-felled area have been logged, leaving a bare slope. Clear-felling can lead to soil erosion and other problems.

Select-felling
Trees that have been chosen for select-felling are felled with chain saws. Tree fellers are often known as lumberjacks.

Logging in action

Logging machines, such as feller bunchers, are used to cut down trees in clear-felling areas. A feller buncher is a type of harvester. Its "arm" grabs a bunch of trees, then cuts them off at the base with a circular saw or shear. The machine then places the cut trees in a stack, ready for their branches to be removed with a delimber. Finally, they are loaded onto trucks and transported to a timber mill.

From logs to woodchips

Once the logs arrive at the mill, they are placed in a bath to rinse away dirt and other impurities. Next, the logs are debarked. This process removes the outer layer of the log while leaving as much wood as possible. The bark can be either burned for fuel or made into garden mulch. The debarked logs are grated into woodchips around 1 inch (2.5 cm) long by mechanical blades. The chips are then sorted according to size, before being moved to a paper mill, where they will be broken down and turned into pulp.

Ready for chipping
A pile of logs waits to be loaded into the chipper. Woodchips are mainly produced from plantation trees or from timber waste, such as branches or offcuts from sawn logs.

Transporting woodchips
A conveyor belt is used to transport woodchips from the chipper to a series of stockpiles. The chips are then loaded into trucks and taken either to a paper mill or the docks to be shipped overseas.

Making particleboard
Particleboard is made by mixing woodchips and flakes together with glue, then forming the mix into a sheet. The sheets are compressed to reduce their thickness, and to harden and set the resin. The boards are then cooled, trimmed, and sanded, ready to be made into furniture.

From woodchips to pulp

At the paper mill, fibers are extracted from the woodchips and separated from each other. This can be done either by crushing the woodchips in a machine, or by heating them in water with chemicals. The chemicals dissolve the parts of the wood that hold the fibers together. Afterward, the chemicals need to be rinsed away. The finished pulp, called stock, looks like mushy soup.

Transformation
Woodchips are cooked in a high-pressure steam cooker with caustic soda. This process helps to dissolve the lignin, which holds the fibers together. Leftover watery black liquid is then separated from the pulp.

Paper mills
Modern paper mills use large amounts of energy, water, and wood. Papermaking machines can be up to 500 feet (152 m) in length, and can produce a sheet of paper 400 inches (10 m) wide. They operate at speeds of more than 60 miles (100 km) per hour.

Waste products
Waste from paper manufacturing contributes
to air and water pollution, and may cause acid rain.

THE PULPING PROCESS

Once the woodchips have been broken down to
form the watery stock, pulp made from recycled
paper can be added if needed.

Damaged paper is recycled back into a mixing machine.

From pulp to paper

Papermaking stock is about 99 percent water. Before it can be turned into paper, the water needs to be removed. To do this, papermakers spray the stock onto a long, wide mesh screen called a wire. Water drips through the wire and fibers in the stock begin to bond together to form a very thin mat. The mat is then squeezed between felt-covered rollers, which absorb even more of the water. The mat passes over a heated drum until it is totally dry—leaving a long sheet of paper.

1 Stock flows over a wire mesh screen. As the water drips through, the fibers form a thin mat.

2 Wet paper passes through felt rollers, before being dried out even more on a heated drum.

That's Amazing!

In 2002, a school student folded a piece of paper in half 12 times in a row. Until then, no one had been able to fold paper more than seven times. Try it yourself!

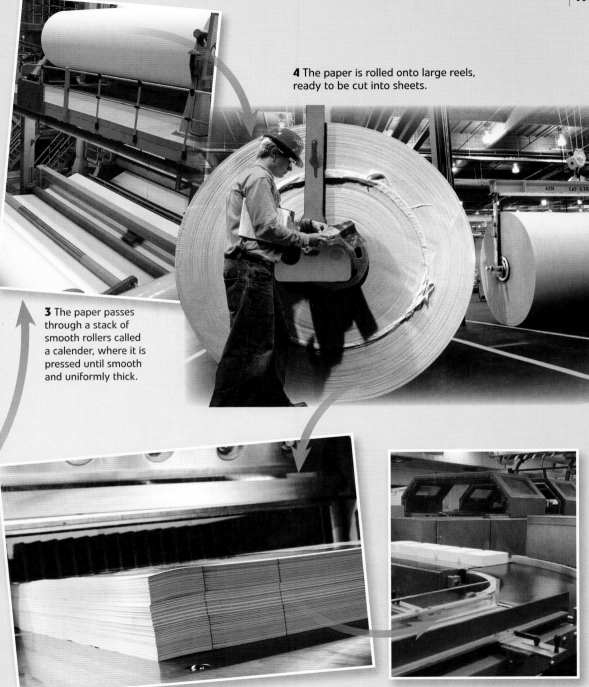

4 The paper is rolled onto large reels, ready to be cut into sheets.

3 The paper passes through a stack of smooth rollers called a calender, where it is pressed until smooth and uniformly thick.

5 The paper is cut to various widths and lengths on a cutting machine.

6 The paper is sorted into piles, ready to be packed into boxes.

Throwaway reading
Every year millions of newspapers and glossy magazines end up in waste dumps.

That's Amazing!
If everyone in the USA recycled just 1 in 10 of the magazines or newspapers they bought, they would save 25 million trees a year.

Sorting wastepaper
At a paper recycling center, the paper is sorted into different grades, then wrapped in bales for transport to the paper mill.

What a waste!

The world produces more than 300 million tons (268 million t) of paper every year. In the USA alone, each year people consume 4 million tons (3.5 million t) of copy paper, 2 billion books, 350 million magazines, and 25 billion newspapers. That is a lot of paper. Add to this the 90 billion pieces of junk mail that end up in people's mailboxes each year and you can see why 40 percent of the trash that ends up in American dumps consists of paper products. It takes between 2 and 4 tons (1.8 and 3.6 t) of trees to produce just 1 ton (0.9 t) of paper. So recycling not only reduces landfills, it also saves trees.

REDUCING WASTE

We can save trees by recycling paper. Some kinds of paper can be recycled several times to make different products. Sixty percent of newspaper is made from recycled paper. Cardboard boxes, too, can be recycled into new ones many times over.

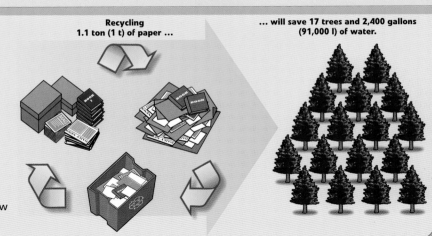

Recycling
1.1 ton (1 t) of paper ...

... will save 17 trees and 2,400 gallons (91,000 l) of water.

Why we should recycle paper

When we recycle paper into new paper products, we use up less of Earth's natural resources. We do not need to cut down as many trees, and, as fewer chemicals are used to make recycled paper, less damage is done to the environment. No pulping is needed, as the wood fibers in recycled paper are already soft.

Animal habitats
Trees and forests provide homes and shelter, and can be a source of food for birds and other animals.

That's Amazing!
The single, oldest living thing on Earth is a bristlecone pine tree in California. This ancient tree is 4,700 years old and was growing when the Egyptians were building the pyramids.

Soil protection
Tree roots help to hold the soil in place and prevent it from being washed away by rainwater.

Water pollution
When wastewater that is drained from pulp is released into rivers and bays, chemicals build up in waterways. This harms fish and plants.

HOW RECYCLING REDUCES POLLUTION

Recycling reduces the amount of dangerous chemicals and gases, such as chlorine and methane, that are released into the environment and put the health of animals, plants, and people at risk.

Landfills
When paper buried in landfills breaks down, it releases methane, a greenhouse gas. Being highly flammable, this gas can also set other waste on fire.

Tree warriors
Carbon dioxide traps heat from the Sun, warming up Earth's atmosphere. Trees take in carbon dioxide, helping to prevent global warming.

Recycled paper products

There are two types of recycling: open-loop and closed-loop. In open-loop recycling, used materials are made into different products, many of which cannot be recycled again. After being recycled several times, the fibers in a product such as an egg carton become too weak to mat together on the papermaking screens. All paper is recycled in an open loop.

Copy paper
High-grade recycled paper products, such as copy paper, are made from a mix of pulp from recycled paper and new pulp.

New products
High-quality products, such as white copy paper

Open-loop recycling
Paper cannot be continuously recycled in the way glass or steel can. Each time paper is reprocessed, its fibers become weaker and shorter. It can be reprocessed only about seven times.

End-of-the-line products
Products that have reached the end of their lifespan and must be thrown away.

CLOSED-LOOP RECYCLING

In closed-loop recycling, a used product, such as an aluminum can or glass bottle, can be remanufactured into the same product over and over again. The materials are never wasted.

Old bottle

No waste
Closed-loop products can be endlessly recycled.

New bottle

Dumping for a good cause
Used glass bottles can be recycled into new glass bottles.

End of the line
The paper in these egg cartons and cardboard rolls has been recycled so many times, these items cannot be recycled again.

Pet litter
An example of a low-grade recycled product is pet litter. No new paper pulp is added to a batch of recycled paper during the manufacturing process.

Plasterboard
Used for walls and ceilings, plasterboard is made from the pulp of recycled paper sandwiched between layers of plaster. It cannot be recycled again.

The recycling process

The recycling process really begins in homes and offices. People collect paper that is no longer needed and put it into recycling containers, ready to be taken to the recycling depot. The paper is sorted into different grades, then taken to the paper mill to be recycled into different products.

1 Collection
Bundles of wastepaper are placed in recycling containers for collection.

2 To the depot
Trucks pick up wastepaper and take it to the recycling depot.

8 Ready to consume
New products are made from the recycled pulp and bought by consumers.

7 Adding
The recycled pulp is added to new paper pulp, then made into paper.

That's Amazing!

Every year, an average office worker in the USA uses around 10,000 sheets of paper, which adds up to about 27 pounds (12.25 kg) per person.

SHREDDED PAPER

Paper is sometimes put through a shredding machine because it contains private information. But shredding paper makes it much more difficult to recycle because the fibers are cut too short. It usually ends up being recycled with other low-grade materials, reducing its usefulness.

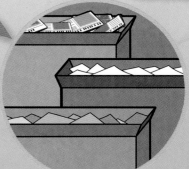

3 Separation
Different types of paper are separated into pure streams of varying grades.

4 To the mill
The paper is pressed into large bundles, then sent to the paper mill.

6 Cleaning
The pulp is put through a screen to remove clips and staples, and cleaned with chemicals to remove ink and glue.

5 Making pulp
The paper is chopped up, then mixed with hot water to form pulp.

Reduce, reuse, rethink

Recycling paper is a great way to save trees, cut down on pollution and waste, and help protect our environment. But there are other things we can do to help with these issues as well. We can reduce our use of paper and paper products. We can reuse them, and rethink the way we use them. To do this can be as simple as writing on both sides of a piece of paper, spreading ripped up newspapers on the garden as mulch, or making paper out of plants such as hemp, rather than wood from trees.

Box of tricks

There are many different ways to reuse cardboard boxes. You can store books or games in them, or rip them up for compost. You can even turn them into a playhouse for your cat or your very own airplane!

Fact or Fiction?

Can paper be made from banana? Yes, it can! In Costa Rica, a company is adding the woody fiber from banana stems to recycled paper pulp to create new banana paper.

Paper versus computers

When using a computer, print out only the documents you really need. Print single-spaced rather than double-spaced. E-mail friends rather than writing to them. When doing projects, bookmark Web pages rather than printing everything out.

Turning paper sludge into fuel

Paper sludge is the waste left over when paper has been recycled so many times it cannot be used again. Normally buried in landfills, this sludge can now be turned into fuel to run papermaking plants.

What you can do

Design a poster that explains the benefits of recycling to your school and community, and gives tips about how to do it.

Here are some ideas to get you started:

1 Provide an eye-catching heading for your poster.

2 Outline some reasons why paper should be recycled.

3 Create a list of the different types of paper that can be recycled. For example, copy paper and newspapers.

4 Provide some examples of different ways people can reduce, reuse, and rethink how they use paper products. For example, using cardboard boxes as storage containers for games.

HINT
You could use some of the material about recycling paper from this book.

Glossary

Aztecs
a group of people who settled in central Mexico in the fourteenth century and rose to become a great power

bales
large bundles

Black Plague
a bubonic plague epidemic in fourteenth-century Europe and Asia. Also known as the Black Death, it killed thousands.

bleached
whitened with chemicals

calender
a machine in which paper or cloth is made smooth and glossy by being pressed through rollers

carbon dioxide
a gas that traps heat in Earth's atmosphere

caustic soda
a strong chemical with burning and corroding qualities that is used in paper manufacturing

compost
a mix of decaying leaves and plants that is used to enrich soil

conveyor belt
a moving track that carries products along from one process to the next

extracted
drawn or pulled out, often with great force or effort

fibers
fine threads

flax
a plant with fibrous leaves

global warming
warming of Earth's atmosphere, which is causing changes in weather patterns

habitat
the type of environment where a plant or animal normally lives

hemp
a plant with fibrous leaves

landfill
a place where waste is buried between layers of earth to build up low-lying land

lignin
a material found in the cell walls of woody plants, which hardens and strengthens them

linen
material made from fibers of the flax plant

logging
cutting down trees for their wood

mulch
a mixture of organic material placed around plants to help suppress weeds, conserve water, and enrich the soil

natural resources
naturally occurring materials, such as wood, that can be processed to make products

origami
the Japanese art of making folded paper models

papyrus
an ancient Egyptian form of paper made from the papyrus plant

plantation
a forest with trees planted to use for timber or to make paper

pulp
the soggy mass of wood fibers that remain when the other parts of the wood are removed

recycling
using old products to make new ones

stock
a sloppy, soupy mixture of wood, pulp, and water

woodchips
small pieces of wood that can be ground to make pulp for papermaking

Index

Credits and acknowledgments

KEY tc=top center; c=center; cr=center right; bl=bottom left; bc=bottom center; br=bottom right; bg=background

CBT = Corbis; GI = Getty Images; iS = istockphoto.com; SH = Shutterstock; TF = Topfoto; TPL = photolibrary.com

front cover bl, bg iS; **back cover** tl iS; c TF; **1**c iS; **2–3**bg TF; **4–5**bg TF; **6**bl, br iS; tr SH; **7**bg iS; **8**tr, cl, bc, cr TF; **9**bc GI; br SH; cl, tl, tr TF; **10**bl CBT; **10–11**bg iS; **11**cr, tl SH; **12**bc, bl TF; **12–13**c TF; **14**bc iS; **14–15**bg TF; **15**br iS; **16–17**tc, bl TF; **17**br CBT; tr TF; **18**br, c CBT; **19**br, tl, tr CBT; bl SH; **20**tl TF; **20–21**br TF; **22**bl iS; tl TF; **22–23**bg iS; **23**br iS; tl, tr TF; **24**tl SH; **24–25**bc iS; **25**c CBT; tr SH; br TF; **27**tr TF; **28–29**bg CBT; **29**tr iS; br TPL; **30**bg SH; **31**bg iS; **32**bg iS

All illustrations copyright Weldon Owen Pty Ltd. **21**tc, **24**c, **25**tc, **26–27**, **30**cr Lionel Portier